ST. GEORGE FOR MERRIE ENGLAND

ST. GEORGE

French, XV. century. South Kensington Museum

Frontispiece

ST. GEORGE FOR MERRIE ENGLAND

by

MARGARET H. BULLEY

WITH FIFTY-SIX FULL-PAGE ILLUSTRATIONS

From an early Norman Tombstone at Conisborough

LONDON: GEORGE ALLEN & SONS
156, CHARING CROSS ROAD
1908

[All rights reserved]

Printed by BALLANTYNE, HANSON & CO.
At the Ballantyne Press, Edinburgh

TO

MY FATHER AND MOTHER

"Why should we talk of Arthur and his knights
Knowing how many men have performed fights!
Or why should we speak of Sir Lancelot du Lake
Or Sir Tristran de Leon that fought for Ladies' sake!
Read old stories over and there you will see
How Saint George, Saint George, he made the dragon flee.
Saint George he was for England, Saint Denis was for France,
Sing HONI SOIT QUI MAL Y PENSE."
—*Old English Ballad*, 1600 (?)

LIST OF CHIEF BOOKS AND PAPERS CONSULTED

Dictionary of Christian Biography. Article by the Rev. G. T. Stokes.
Lives of the Saints. The Rev. S. Baring-Gould.
Curious Myths of the Middle Ages. Rev. S. Baring-Gould.
The Martyrdoms and Miracles of St. George. Oriental Text series, No. 1. Dr. E. Wallis Budge.
Journal of the Archæological Institute. 1900. Article by Mr. Lewis André.
List of Buildings with Mural Decorations. Keyser.
Fors Clavigera. J. Ruskin.
The Life of St. George. Dr. Clapton.
Norfolk Archæology. Vol. III.
Encyclopédie Théologique.
Horus et Saint Georges. M. Clermont Ganeau.
Zur Georgslegende. M. Huber.
History of Reading. Coates.
The Coventry Pageants. Ed. Sharp.
St. George of Cappadocia. Peter Heleyn. 1631.
The Most Famous History of the Seven Champions of Christendom. Richard Johnstone. 1601.
The Order of the Ceremonies used at Windsor, 1671.
Records of the Borough of Leicester, 1327–1509.
Sarum Missal.
Fabyan's Chronicle. Ed. Ellis.
History of the World, 1617. Sir W. Raleigh. Ed. of 1676.
Sir Bevys of Hampton.
Archæologia. Several volumes.
Publications of the Camden Society.
Publications of the Surtees Society.
Publications of the Chetham Society.
Publications of the Percy Society.

St. George for Merrie England

THE GOLDEN LEGEND

AMONG all the stories of St. George there is no greater favourite than that of the fight with the dragon. Artists have painted and carved it for our delight, musicians and poets have celebrated it in song and verse, and it has duly taken its place in the literature of the world.

In olden times, however, this charming fairy story was implicitly believed by the people. The history of St. George was so shrouded in mystery that, perhaps not unnaturally, Romance stepped in, and during the course of centuries legends grew up around the Saint's name which were more symbolic than accurate. The earliest form of the full-grown legend is found in the celebrated "Legenda Aurea," which was written by Jaques de Voragine, Archbishop of Geneva, who lived from 1236 to 1298 A.D. It was translated into English by Caxton, and it is this version that shall first be quoted from and described, as it has always been the most popular. This is how the story runs.

Long ago there was a city in Libya called Selene. Now the people of that city were in great trouble because a terrible dragon, which was ravaging the country round, had made its lair in a marshy swamp near the city walls. Its poisonous breath reached the people, who had all fled for safety into the city, and pestilence began to spread rapidly among them.

To make it keep farther away, they gave it a daily offering of two sheep, and for some time all went well; but the day came when the last sheep had been devoured. Long and anxiously the people discussed what was to be done. The dragon's breath was fast spreading sickness among them, and steps had to be taken at once to appease its

St. George for Merrie England

wrath. At last they reluctantly decided that lots must be drawn among the children under fifteen, and that each day one must be sacrificed to the cruel monster.

Then came a day when the lot fell on the King's little daughter, the Princess Cleodolinda.

With tears and prayers he implored that her life should be spared. "For the love of Goddes take golde and sylver and alle that I have, and lete me have my doughter." But the people only answered that what was just for them was just for him, and that they could only allow him eight days in which to mourn and prepare his daughter. "Your doughter shal be gyven or ellys we shal brenne you and your hous." Thus came their stern answer.

So the eight days passed.

"Thenne dyd the Kyng doo araye his doughter lyke as she shold be wedded and embraced hyr, kyssed hir, and gave hir his benedyccion, and after ledde hyr to the place where the dragon was."

Now as she wandered along, the tears running down her cheeks, who should ride by but a tribune of the Roman army, one George of Cappadocia, a valiant knight and true.

Seeing her tears, he stopped his beautiful white horse, and asked her the cause of her distress; but she only answered, "Goo ye your waye fayre younge man that ye perysshe not also." When he still questioned her, and would not go until she answered him, she then described the sad fate that had befallen her. "Fayre doughter doubte ye nothing herof, for I shal helpe the in the name of Jhesu Cryste," answered George of Cappadocia.

Hardly had he spoken when the dragon crawled out of the marsh, and came rushing towards them.

The tribune wheeled round his horse, and, commending himself to God, charged again and again at the monster, finally transfixing it with his spear.

Then he turned to the poor little Princess, who with trembling and tears had watched the fight. "Delyver to me your gyrdel, and bynde hit about the necke of the dragon, and be not aferd." This she did, and we are told, "when she had doon soo, the dragon folowed hyr as it had been a meke beest and debonayr."

The Golden Legend

So they came back together to the city; but when the people saw the dragon they began to fly to the hills, and would not come back until St. George had promised to cut off its head before them all in the market-place. So this was done, and four carts drawn by oxen bore away the hated beast. Such was the joy of the people in the victory of St. George and his faith, that the King, Queen, and Princess, and twenty thousand of their subjects, not counting women and children, were baptized and became Christians. The King would have given his daughter and half his kingdom to St. George, but he only answered that he must go on his way, and begging "that he shold have charge of the churches, that he shold honaire the preestes and here theyr serruyce dylygently, and that he shold have pyte on the poure peple," he kissed the King and departed.

So over the hills and far away he went, and not very long after that time the Emperor Diocletian, under whom St. George was serving, began to persecute the Christians. St. George openly defied the Emperor, and publicly proclaimed himself to be a Christian, whereupon Dacian the Governor had him thrown into prison, and tortured many times, saying, "I shal deye for angrey if I may not surmounte & ouercome thys man;" but from all his wounds he was miraculously healed and saved. Finally his head was cut off, and so died St. George, a martyr to his faith.

This, then, is the earliest version of the full-grown legend. There are also two other early records; one the Breviary Service for St. George's Day, as it existed before its revision by Pope Clement VII., and secondly, an old Norman tombstone at Conisborough in Yorkshire, in which the figure of the Princess is first met with in art. The hog-backed shape of the stone is generally considered to show Scandinavian influence, but the kite-shaped shield and conical caps are undoubtedly Norman, and it has been dated as early twelfth century work. This Conisborough stone has the interesting detail that the Princess is already in the dragon's clutches: an abbot is blessing the exploit of the Saint.

St. George for Merrie England

THE "ACTS"

The latter part of the story of St. George, as we read it in the Golden Legend, was evidently founded on the early Greek and Coptic Acts. These Acts professed to give the true history of the Saint; but as every fresh version that appeared was wilfully corrupted by its transcribers, even as early as the year 494 A.D., they were pronounced by Pope Gelasius to be entirely fabulous. On the other hand, Theodosius, Bishop of Jerusalem, and Theodotus, Bishop of Ancyra, both used and accepted the earliest version, which was written by Pasikrates, the servant of St. George. We know that a Syriac version of this work existed in the sixth century, and it has much in common with the Coptic texts. The Ethiopian Acts (which numbered eighty miracles), and also the Latin and Arabic, were of a later date.

The Coptic texts have been edited and translated by Dr. E. Wallis Budge from several old manuscripts. Two of the most important are by Pasikrates, who has been already mentioned, and Theodosius, Bishop of Jerusalem; and it is on some such accounts as these that the Greek texts by Simeon Malaphrastes, Andrew of Crete, and Gregory of Cyprus are based.

They tell us that George was a native of Melitene in the east of Cappadocia. His grandfather was John, chief governor of Cappadocia, and his parents were Anastasius, governor of Melitene, and Kira Theognosta, who was daughter of Dionysius, the Count of Lydda Diospolis. All of them were Christians. George, wishing for advancement, set out for Tyre, where he intended to ask the Emperor Diocletian to make him a count. On his arrival, however, he was so disgusted with the idolatry that prevailed in the country that, giving away his money and jewels, and dismissing his servants, he demanded an audience with Dadiamus the governor, and proclaimed himself a Christian.

The result was that Dadiamus ordered him to be tortured in every conceivable way; but after every fresh torture he was miraculously healed by Christ. The Governor then invited any one who had the power, to destroy him. Athanasius, a magician, came forward, and

The "Acts"

gave him poisoned drinks, pronouncing the names of powerful demons as he did so; but these failed to harm George, and Athanasius himself was converted to Christianity. George was then tortured again and again, but every time he was miraculously restored by Christ and His angels. He then wrought four miracles. He raised to life a dead ox belonging to a poor widow called Cholastike, and later some men and women who had been buried for more than two hundred years; he caused the pillar of a widow's house to take root and become a tree; and lastly, he made the lame and blind son of a widow both walk and see.

Dadiamus then had him burnt, but the winds brought back his ashes, and he lived again. He was then tortured and thrown into prison, but Christ appeared and healed his wounds. Then came seven years of tortures, but when these had no effect Dadiamus offered to kiss him and make peace, but St. George refused. He then converted Alexandra the Queen. The following day he was ordered to bring sacrifices to Apollo, whereupon he commanded the widow's son whom he had healed to go into the temple and bid the idol to come down. When the devil who inhabited the idol heard the command he leapt from the pedestal, and George struck the ground, which opened and swallowed him. When he was again ordered to pray to false gods, he asked for help from heaven, and fire and thunder came down and destroyed the temple. Then again came tortures, and when he again recovered from them, seventy governors, including Dadiamus, signed his death warrant, whereupon George prayed to heaven, and they were all consumed by fire when at meat.

He was finally beheaded at Pharmuthi, and his three servants took his body and laid it outside the city, whence it was taken to Joppa and then to Lydda. His brother Andrew started to build a shrine over the place where the Saint's house stood, in which to place the body, but became discouraged because of the expense, whereupon George appeared in a vision and showed him a spot where he had hidden money during his lifetime.

This is a summary of the Coptic texts, which, according to Dr. Wallis Budge, must have been known and read in the early part of the sixth century. Dr. Budge suggests that the story of St. George overcoming the hated dragon had its origin in the Saint's defeat of the wicked governor Dadiamus, and that Alexandra, the wife of Diocletian, who suffered martyrdom, is the original of the Princess Cleodolinda. As far as other testimony goes, we can safely identify Dadiamus, the "great governor of the Persians," with Galerius Valerius Maximianus, who reigned jointly with Diocletian and was noted for his extraordinary cruelty. It is also known that Diocletian published two edicts at Nicomedia; one against the property of Christians, and one against their lives, and this exactly agrees with the statement in the Coptic texts.

These Acts, however, were not the only versions of this many-sided legend. Another insists that before St. George fought his famous fight with the dragon he had been killed by the Gauls, and that the Virgin herself had raised him again to life. This is why he was so often called her knight or champion, and painted kneeling by her side. Again we hear that he accepted the King's offer, and married the Princess, and that they lived happily ever after. Also that he fought with the Moors, captured their king, and reigned in his place. Then we are told that Sabra, or Aja, was the real name of the Princess, or else Elya, the name she is known by in the Scandinavian version of the legend. Also, needless to remark, many and various were the places that claimed to be the scene of St. George's birth, death, and fight with the dragon.

THE TRUE ST. GEORGE

Of the true history of St. George very little is known. When we turn to the few accurate and early accounts which have come down to us, we find that there are two claimants to the title. According to the generally accepted version, St. George was born at Lydda about the year 270 A.D., and was martyred at Nicomedia in 303. In the writings of Eusebius, a contemporary of St. George, who was Bishop of Constantinople in the year 338, the following entry is found (I quote the translation given by the Rev. S. Baring-Gould):—

"Immediately on the promulgation of the edict (of Diocletian) a certain man of no mean origin, but highly esteemed for his temporal

The True St. George

dignities, as soon as the decree was published against the churches in Nicomedia, stimulated by a divine zeal and excited by an ardent faith, took it as it was openly placed and posted up for public inspection, and tore it to shreds as a most profane and wicked act. This, too, was done when the two Cæsars were in the city, the first of whom was the eldest and chief of all, and the other held fourth grade of the imperial dignity after him. But this man, as the first that was distinguished there in this manner, after enduring what was likely to follow an act so daring, preserved his mind, calm and serene until the moment when his spirit fled." This nameless martyr has been generally supposed to be St. George.

The second claimant is the "Holy George" mentioned in the following entry in the "Chronicon Pascali," an historical document which was compiled by three people, the first of whom carried it down to the year A.D. 354, the second to 629, and the third to 1042. The sentence runs: "In the year 255 of the ascension of our Lord a persecution of the Christians took place and many suffered martyrdom, among whom also the Holy George was martyred."[1]

This mention then of a "Holy George" may be all we actually know of our Patron Saint. There are also two other documents which, though not of such early dates as the two previously mentioned, are still interesting as possibly throwing further light on this perplexing subject. The first is a *Syriac Martyrologium* (published by Assemani in Syriac), in which there is no record of the actual name of St. George, but on the 24th of April, one day after the recognised date of the martyrdom, there is a note which reads, "April 24th. Anthimus . . . and five other confessors" (confessor meant "witness of faith" when used in this sense). There is a space after the name of "Anthimus" which might very possibly have held the missing name of George. As a further clue, there is an old Byzantine chronicle by a writer of the tenth century, Georgius Cedrenus, where he gives a brief account of this very persecution, and mentions the name of George as a victim of it.

---

[1] Mr. Baring-Gould, whose translation I again quote, discusses the date at length. See "Lives of the Saints," vol. iv. p. 308.

St. George for Merrie England

The second is the *Martyrologium Hieronymianum*, a manuscript in the Berne Museum, which was written in the eighth or ninth century. In it the name of George is mentioned three times; on April 23rd, 24th, and 25th, as representing the days of his passion and the day of his feast. Duchesne considers that this manuscript represents an older compilation than the Syriac.

Then again, in recent years, a very important and interesting discovery has been made. Burckhardt when travelling in Syria found two early churches, one in Ezra, one in Shaka, each of which had old Greek dedications inscribed to St. George. Mr. Hogg has discussed them at great length in the "Transactions of the Royal Literary Society," and by most acute argument shows that both are very early dedications, and one must have been made in the year 346 —that is, within fifty years of St. George's death.

This becomes very important testimony when we turn to the famous charge made against St. George by Dr. Reynolds of Norwich, and later again by the historian Gibbon, who seemed to delight in confusing him with that other George of Cappadocia, the Arian of infamous repute, who was Bishop of Alexandria until the year 361 A.D.

THE FALSE ST. GEORGE

Ammianus Marcellinus, a contemporary authority, tells us that this George, a man of very humble parentage, was born in a fuller's mill at Epiphania in Cilicia, and made a living by selling bacon to the army at Constantinople. When it was discovered that his great profits were made by no honest means, he fled to Cappadocia, and there adopted the profession of Arianism, which was in favour at court at that time. His quick wits, and readiness to aid others in schemes perhaps none too honest, soon made him popular among a certain set. He collected a large library, won a reputation as a savant, and was finally chosen as archbishop and raised to the throne of Athanasius. His reign was one of tyranny and oppression. He persecuted Pagans and Christians alike, acquired the monopoly of

The False St. George

nitre, salt, paper, and even funerals, and half ruined the Alexandrian merchants. The time came when the people could bear it no longer. They had the tyrant thrown into prison, and there he remained until, after twenty-four days, the heathen multitude forced the doors and, after tearing his body to pieces, flung it into the sea.

This, then, is the man that Gibbon says "has been transformed into the renowned St. George of England, the patron of arms, of chivalry, and of the Garter." He tells us that the rival of Athanasius was dear and sacred to the Arians, and that his meritorious death finally obliterated the memory of his life. In after years his partisans, taking advantage of the fact that both Saint and bishop were Georges of Cappadocia, inserted into the current Acts the name of George the Arian and other matter concerning his life, and in this way the slander spread. As a conclusive proof against this slander we need only quote the discovery of Burckhardt which shows that of the two churches previously alluded to, one was dedicated to St. George in the year 346—that is, during the lifetime of George the Arian, who died in 362. If further evidence were necessary, we have the Chronicle of Hesychius Milesius, written in the year 518 A.D., in which we read that Constantine the Great dedicated a church in Constantinople to St. George the Martyr, about the year 330 A.D. This again was during the lifetime of the Arian George.

It is extraordinary how this theory can ever have gained ground. The Coptic Acts were known and read early in the fifth century, and they contain no allusion to the Arian. From the earliest times there has always been the record of the "Holy George," and it is impossible that the worship of the Saint, which dated from his martyrdom, should have been offered to any one so infamous as George the Arian. Among other early records of St. George, we have the decree of Pope Gelasius in 494 A.D., which has already been alluded to; the Book of Martyrs of St. Gregory of Tours in the sixth century, which mentions him; the beautiful poem of Venantius Fortunatus, written in his honour in the year 500 A.D., and the dedication of the Velabro church in Rome by Leo II. in the year 682 A.D. The church built over the tomb of St. George at Lydda (which existed, until recent years, in a ruinous state) has, from the earliest times, been called the

St. George for Merrie England

work of Constantine. Also, when, at the end of the sixth century, the Bagratides ascended the throne of Georgia, they took for their arms, as well as other Christian subjects, that of St. George killing the dragon.

There can be no doubt, after these early proofs and acknowledgments, that George the Martyr lived and died, and we can only agree with Fuller, who in 1634 wrote naïvely "that it is impossible that our English nation, amongst so many saints that were, would choose one that was not to be their patroné, especially seeing the world in their age had rather a glut than a famine of saints."

WRITERS ON ST. GEORGE

To denounce St. George, or to confuse him with other persons, has always had a strange fascination for men. Calvin announced that he did not believe in his existence. A hundred years later Dr. Reynolds of Norwich wrote to the same effect, and Dr. Pettingal and Mr. Byrom followed suit in 1753. Among several books and papers written in defence of the Saint, Peter Heleyn's book, published in 1633, is perhaps the most interesting and amusing. It is called "The History of that most famous Saint and Soldier of Christ Isus, St. George of Cappadocia," and it undertook "to cleere the history of St. George from all further questions."

It begins with a little dissertation on the folly of those who "in this more neat and curious age, do peevishly (to say no worse) reject those ancient stories which are commended to us in the best and gravest authors. I say not this to blunt the edge of any vertuous endeauors," the author continues, "not so—only I sayd it a little to take doune, if possible, that height of selfe-conceit and stomacke wherewith too many of us doe affront those worthies of the former dayes." He then proceeds to tell the story of the Saint, and it is amusing to see how, in his heart of hearts, even though evidently a little ashamed of his credulity, he still has an inclination to believe in the fight with the dragon.

"Strabo," he says, "relates it out of *Possidonius* that a dead

Writers on St. George

serpent was once found in Syria of that wondrous bignesse that two horsemen standing on each side of it could not see each other. And our own chronicles, to go no further, make mention somewhere of a dragon of almost incredible greatnesse found at Hooke-Norton, not faire from Oxen, besides what Hoveden hath reported '*de serpentibus in Sussevia visis magna cum admiratione*' of serpents seen in Sussex, to the great astonishment of the people. Such creatures there are and have beene in being in most places; so in *Africa* especially there where Saint George is said to have killed a dragon . . . an *African* or *Lybian* dragon, for so is reported in the *Legend*. So," as he gravely sums up, "why might not *George*, a soldier both of great magnanimity and discretion, God's love and goodnesse concurring with him in the act, bee said to kill a Dragon, a serpentine creature of great bulke and danger."

This theory is to a certain extent supported by modern writers on St. George, who suggest that the fight with the dragon may not have been a symbol alone, but an actual combat with a crocodile or some such creature.

Peter Heleyn is very angry with all authors of false versions of the story, and has scant pity for Richard Johnstone, who wrote "The Famous Historie of the Seven Champions of Christendome," in which St. George is said to be born in England and of English blood. Much abuse is also heaped on the heads of "those Heretickes and atheists who deprave the story of our blessed saynt George the Martyr by mingling with it some passages of special note occurring in the life of an Arian Bishop of that name, then George of Alexandria." He also quotes[1] that "bytwene Jherusalem and porte Japhe by a towne callyd Ramys is a chapell of Saynt George whiche is now desolate and uncouered and therein dwelle Crysten Crekys. And in the sayd chapel lyeth the body of saynt George but not the heed. And there lyen hys fader and moder and hys uncle not in the chapel but under the walls of the chapel," which charmingly expressed bit of information we need not necessarily believe. One cannot help feeling also that relations form quite an unnecessary part of a saint's economy, such radiant and isolated beings generally rising above mere family ties, and certainly family vaults!

[1] From "Golden Legend."

St. George for Merrie England

It is interesting to know what Sir Walter Raleigh had to say about St. George. In his " History of the World," after mentioning the old castle of St. George five miles from Ptolomaio, he continues, " and though for the credit of St. George killing the Dragon I leave every man to his own belief, yet I cannot but think that, if the Kings of England had not some probable record of that his memorable act among many others ; it was strange that the order full of honour which Edward III. founded, and which his successors royally have continued should have borne his name, seeing the world had not that scarcity of saints in those days as the English were driven to make such an erection upon a fable or person feigned."

He then quotes Adrichomius first in Latin and then in English. "In this place which by the inhabitants is called Cappadocia, not far from Berytus, men say that the famous knight of Christ, St. George, did rescue the king's daughter from a huge dragon, and, having killed the beast, delivered the virgin to her parent. In memory of which deed a church was after built there. If this authority suffice not," Raleigh continues, "we may rather make the story allegorical, figuring the victory of Christ, than accept of George the Arian bishop mentioned by Marcellinus." It is interesting to see in one of the old maps of Adrichomius, dated 1558, that a little engraving of St. George killing the dragon marks the reputed scene of the fight on the somewhat curious coast of Africa.

Richard Johnstone's "Famous History of the Seven Champions of Christendome," a book already alluded to, has been the cause of an immense amount of confusion on the subject of St. George. It was written in 1608, and was largely taken from an old poem called "Sir Bevys of Hampton," which had been famous since the time of Chaucer.

To parts of this story, current English versions of St. George's legend were evidently added, with the result that confusion was indeed worse confounded. We are told that St. George was born in Coventry, and was the son of Lord Albert, High Steward of that town. At the birth of this extraordinary child a "bloody crosse" was found on his right hand and upon his left leg a golden garter, and his subsequent adventures were as strange as his early decorations. His mother died at his birth, and not long afterwards he was stolen from careless servants

Writers on St. George

by the enchantress Kalyb, "a bitter enemy to true nobility." For seven years she kept him prisoner, together with the other champions of Christendom, but after that time they escaped and scattered over the world, meeting with many and strange adventures. St. George went to Egypt, where a hermit told him about the dragon, and after killing it and undergoing still further adventures, including fights with the Saracens, he overcame Almedor the Blackamor king of Morocco, and, helped by the other champions, was set on the throne in his place. He finally married the Sultan of Egypt's daughter, and took her back to Coventry, where they had three sons and lived happily ever after.

Such are the outlines of a book which coloured a greater part of the subsequent literature upon St. George. We may also quote Peter Heleyn, who remarks: "To this relation of his being born of English parentage our admir'd *Spencer*, although poetically, doth seem to give some countenance," as certain well-known verses quoted in the following pages will show. This version lingered long among the country districts of England, which is perhaps only natural when our ignorant objections to a foreigner are remembered. How much more delightful to be able to claim our national Saint as English born! In 1757 Bishop Pococke, writing from Highworth, tells how the peasants took him to "Dragon Hill," and showed him a bare spot where grass would never grow because of the dragon's blood shed in the famous fight with St. George. They also told him that the white horse cut out of the chalk on the hillside was the Saint's white charger.

Denmark also claims to be the scene of the fight, and the story only differs in the respect that, instead of two sheep, two eggs were given daily to the dragon, which certainly represents him as the possessor of a more dainty and epicurean appetite than his Lybian fellow. When the supply of eggs began to give out, one egg and one human being were offered, but otherwise the story is the same.

In the East, St. George is honoured by both Christian and Moslem, and from the earliest times the Greek Church has designated him "the Great Martyr," the "Victorious One," and "Trophy-bearer." He is the Patron Saint of Germany, Portugal, Barcelona, Genoa, Ferrara Armenia, Antioch, Constantinople, various parts of France, and of the Coptic Christians. "St. George for Holy Russia" is the battle-cry of

St. George for Merrie England

the Czar, even as "St George for Merrie England" spurred on our tired soldiers. He is the patron of nine military orders, and is generally considered the protector of all soldiers and sailors. We read, too, that the old French order of knighthood was given by the King with the words, "Je te fais chevalier, au nom de Dieu et de Monseigneur Saint George, pour la foi et justice loyalment gardes et l'Eglise, femmes, veuves, et orphelins défender."

THE CULT IN ENGLAND

Our first knowledge of St. George must have been brought from the East, by the Christian missionaries sent by Pope Gregory in 597 A.D. It has been stated that St. George visited England while serving under Diocletian, and that that is how St. George's Channel came by its name, but nothing has yet been found to prove the theory.

In the testimony of Adamnan we get a very early mention of the Saint. He tells how Arculf was returning to his French bishopric in the year 701 A.D., when he was carried to Iona by adverse winds. There he was cared for by Adamnan, to whom he dictated his adventures, and among them we find the following paragraph :—" St. Arcolfus also told us another reliable story about George the Martyr, which he indisputably taught in the city of Constantinople."

From Arculf's travels it is most probable that Bede got his knowledge of St. George, and in consequence entered his name for April 23 in his calendar, and through him the knowledge would have spread among the monks.

Then in Anglo-Saxon literature we have three references to the Saint. Once in a very early Ritual of the church of Durham, assignable to the beginning of the ninth century; once in a Martyrology belonging to Corpus Christi College, Cambridge, which was given by Bishop Leofric to the Cathedral Church of Exeter, early in the eleventh century; and once in the ancient Anglo-Saxon "Passion of St. George," written by Aelfric, Archbishop of York during 1023–1051, and belonging to the Cambridge University Library. Tradition also says that King Arthur chose St. George as the patron of the Knights of the Round Table.

The Cult in England

But although St. George was reverenced in England in Anglo-Saxon times, it was Richard I. who first brought his cult to England, and Edward III. who raised it to that great height of popularity which it held for so long. Even before that time, William of Malmesbury tells us that during the battle of Antioch, on June 28, 1087, when the Crusaders were hard pressed by the Saracens, the martyrs George and Demetrius were seen "hastily approaching from the mountainous districts hurling darts against the enemy but assisting the Franks." This greatly encouraged the soldiers, among whom were many Normans under Robert, son of William the Conqueror, and no doubt through them the popularity of St. George began to grow in England.

The story runs, that Richard I., when fighting the Holy War in Palestine, also beheld the radiant figure of St. George in shining armour and a red cross, leading the armies on to victory. We know that Richard repaired the church of St. George at Lydda when in Palestine, and he certainly returned to England full of enthusiasm for the warrior Saint. In the reign of his nephew, Henry III., in 1220, St. George's name was passed into the calendar for April 23, and two years later it was decreed by the National Council of Oxford that the day should be kept as a festival of lesser rank.

Edward I. had the red cross of St. George displayed upon his banner together with the arms of St. Edmund and St. Edward the Confessor, the former Patron Saint of England. Then came the reign of Edward III. The Order of the Garter was founded in 1330, "in the honour of God, our Lady, and St. George." It is interesting to know that the order originally included ladies, who were known as "dames de la confraternité de St. George." In 1347, at the siege of Calais, the King, moved by some sudden impulse, drew his sword, crying "Ha! St. Edward! Ha! St. George!" so inspiring his troops that they renewed their charge with fresh courage and triumphantly won the day, and after this time St. George may be said to have supplanted St. Edward as our national Saint. In 1348, a year later, the chapel of Windsor was dedicated to him.

Then in 1386, in the reign of Richard II., during the invasion of Scotland, the King ordained that every man should "bere a signe of the armes of St. George, large, bothe before and behynde." The red cross

St. George for Merrie England

was worked on a white cassock or coat which was worn over the armour, and it became "a seemly and magnificent thing to see the armies of the English so sparkle like the rising sun."

In 1399 came another important change. At the Synod held at St. Paul's under Archbishop Arundel, the clergy presented a petition desiring that "the feast of St. George the Martyr, who is the spiritual patron of the soldiery of England, should be appointed to be solemnized throughout England and observed as a holiday, even as other nations observe the feast of their own patron."

In the reign of Henry V., Chicheley, Archbishop of Canterbury, ordained that St. George's Day should be kept as one of the feasts of greater rank, taking its place with Christmas Day and Easter, and that an entire holiday should be given to the people in its honour. "An English Chronicle" (Camden Soc.) gives us the following interesting account of the beginning of the battle of Agincourt in 1415: "And anon euery Englishe manne knelid doun and put a litille porcion of erthe in his mouth, and thanne saide the King with an highe vois 'In the name of Almygte God and of St. George avaunt baner, and St. George this day thym helpe.' Thane the two bataillez mette togider and fouzten sore and long time, but almyzte God and St. George fouzten that day for us and graunted our King the victory."

If we hunt through old state and civic records and corporation and church accounts, we find endless references to the cult of St. George. Masses, feasts, processions, tourneys, and races were held in honour of his day; guilds bearing his name were established, and much money and thought were expended in preparing numberless St. Georges and Cleodolindas, chargers and dragons, to take their part in pageants and ceremonies. Chief among these were the celebrations at Windsor, which were held annually on St. George's Day. There was first a service at the chapel, at which all the Knights of the Garter were obliged to be present, then special tourneys, and lastly a great feast as a fitting end to the festivities. In William Gregory's "Chronicle of London" we get an interesting account of one of these feasts. In this instance it was deferred until the visit of the Emperor Sigismund, who was bringing with him as an offering to King Henry V. the so-called heart of St. George, a precious relic. It may

The Cult in England

be mentioned in explanation, that a "sotellete" was a representation of some scene made in pastry and highly coloured. This is how the account runs:—

"Ande thys yere com the Emperowre of Almayne in to London be-fore the Feste of Syn Georg. Ande the feste was deferryde unto hys commynge, & that was done solempny at the castylle of Wyndesore... Ande at the mete the kyng sate on the right syde of the emperour ande the Duke of Bedford sate on the lefte syde... Ande the fyrste sotellete of the fyrste cours was howe Oure Lady armyd Syn George and a aungylle doyng on his sporys. Ande the secunde sotellete was syn George rydynge and fyghtyng whythe a dragon whythe hys spere in hys honde. And the iij sotellete was a castelle & Syn Geors & the kynges doughter ledyng the lambe at the castelle gatys. And all thes sotelleteys were servyd be-fore the emperorure & the kyng & noo ferthe ande othyr lordys were servyd with sotelleteys aftyr hyr astate & degre."

In Fabyan's Chronicle there is another allusion to a sotellete, this time prepared for the coronation feast of Henry VI., when "kynge Henry beynge upon the age of ix yeres was solempnly crowned in Seynt Peters church of Westmynster... and after that solempnzacion the sayd church fynysshed, an honourable feest in the great halle of Westmynster was kepte.... Between the third course was a sotyltie of our Lady syttynge with her childe in her lappe and she holdyng a crowne in her hande. Seynt George and Seynt Denys knelynge on eyther syde presentyd to her kyng Henryes fygure berynge in hande this balade as foloweth:

> O blessyd Lady, Cristys moder dere
> And thou seynt George that called art her Knyght."

William Gregory's Chronicle tells us that during this feast "at the fyrste course they came doune & wente by fore the kyngys champyon Syr Phylyppe Dymmoke that rode in the halle i-armyde clene as Syn Jorge. And he proclaymyd... that the kynge was ryghtefulle ayre to the crowne of Ingelonde... & that he was redy for to defende hyt as hys knyghte & hys champyon."

Then in the reign of Henry VII. we come across another proof of

St. George for Merrie England

the great veneration in which St. George was held, Fabyan's Chronicle again being our authority. It tells how "upon Saynt Georges day the Kyng went in procession in Poules church where was shewn a legge of Saynt George closed in sylver whych was newly sent to the kyng." We can tell how this relic was prized by the King, for in his will of 1509 we read: "Also we give and bequeathe ... the precious relique of oon of the leggs of Saint George set in silver parcell gilte, which came to the hands of our broder and cousyn Loys of ffraunce the tyme that he wan and recover'd the citie of Millein, and was geven and sent to us by our cousyne the cardinal of Amboys legate of Fraunce: the which pece of the holie Crosse and leg of Saincte George we wol bee set upon the said aulter for the garnishing of the same upon all principal and solempne fests."

The most important of the Guilds of St. George were those at Chichester, Leicester, Coventry, and Norwich. The earliest reference to the Chichester Guild is in an old public deed of 1394—the seventeenth year of the reign of Richard II. The Leicester Guild was of later date, for we first hear of it in the early part of the fifteenth century. It was of considerable importance, and held its meetings in the Guild Hall and its services in the chapel of St. George, which occupied a corner of St. Martin's Church. Near the altar of the chapel was a raised platform on which stood a life-sized figure of St. George on horseback, clad in gorgeous armour. Once a year this figure was drawn round the town in the great procession called "The Ryding of the George," in which the Mayor and Corporation and all the townsfolk were obliged to take part. At one time, however, this custom must have fallen into abeyance, for in an old deed of 1523 we read, "Whosoeur be the maister of Seynt Georgis Gylde shall cause the George to be rydyn according to the olde aunciant costome y[at] ys to sey betwyx Sent Georgys day and Wytsondey."

The Coventry Guild was celebrated for the part it played in the city pageants. We get the following reference to it in an old city Leet Book, which describes the pageant prepared in honour of Prince Edward upon his entry into the city in 1476:—"Upon the Condite in the Crosse Chepyng was Seint George crowned & kynges dought[r] knelyng afore hym w[t] a lambe & the fader & the moder beyng in a toure a

The Cult in England

boven, beholdyng Seint George savyng their dought[r] from the dragon. And the Condite rennyng wyne in iiij placez, and mynstralcy of Orgonpleyinge & Seint George havyng this speeche under wryttyn:

> "O myghty God our all secour celestiall
> Which his Reyne has geven to dower
> To thi moder and to me George pteccion ppetual
> Hit to defende from enemies ffere & nere
> And as this mayden defended was here
> Bi thy grace from this Dragon devour
> So lorde ps've this noble prynce : & ev' be his sucour."

We can get a vivid picture of the Norwich Guild from its ancient charter, which is still preserved. The following extracts show us what an important body it was, and how it dominated the life of the town.

"In the worschepe of the Fader Sone & the Holy Goost and of owre Lady Seynt Mary and of the Glorious Martyr Seynt George and all Goddes Holy. There was begonne a Fraternite the yer of our Lorde MCCCXXIII . . . qwerfore that seing diverse personys wel wylled & styrred to devocion of the glorious Martyr forseid, soghten & porsueden wyth grete labour and besynes to the King for grace to continew her devocion, & to have the name of Fraternite & Gujld of Brether'n & Sistern of Seynt George for hem and her successors evermor withoute ende to endurn. . . .

"It is ordeined be the comōn ascent of the Fraternite that all the Brethern and Susteren of the Fraternite shullen halwen the day of Seynt George yerely on what day so it befalle.

"Also ther kepe her dyvine servise of both even-songes and messe in the cathedral forseide & other observaunces of the Fraternite ordeyned . . . be assent of the bretheren yer schul ordeyne and pfix a day on which day alle bretheren & susteren schull kepen all her observaunces of her Divine Service aforn reherced & kepe her Riding & haven and kepen & weren her Clothing & holden her Fest. . . .

"Also it is ordeyned that the alderman and maystres schul assigne a Day for asemble before the day of Seint George on qwiche day thoo XXIIII or the more part of hem schul chesen her George & a Man

St. George for Merrie England

to bere his swerd and be his kerver to for him. And a man to bere the bāner of Seynt George and tweye Men to ber the wax or do bern with honest persones and to go with hem. . . .

"And at that assemble the alderman and maystres schul make relacyon and knowyng at qwat place the bretheren and susteren schul gaddre for her Ryding, And at qwat place the bretheren and susteren schul felten her wax & in qwat place thei schul ete togedre . . . also it is ordeyned on the day of Seint George or elles another day assigned as it beforn reherced, that every Brother schal be in his levery for that yer on horsbak at certayn place be on ower & tyme assigned. . . .

"Also qwan the reding is don that every brother and syster be redy at the place be forn assegned at setting and beryng her wax, ond offren it up at the heye awter of the churche forseid in worchepe of the Trinite, oure Lady & of the Glorious Martyr Seint George, ther to brenne. . . .

"Also it is ordeined qwan the messe is seid & onded all the bretheren and susteren schul gon honestle to her mete to place assegned by the alderman & the maystres and then for to ete togedre every brother and suster paying for her Mete Wax & Minestral xd."

In old books of church accounts we find numberless references to St. George. "Payd for brokyng down the walle where Seynt George standeth 6d." "For irrennys & wyer to the table of Seynt George 6d." "Paid for makinge St. Georgs candlestick 2s." "For dressing & harnessing Seint George harness 6s. 8d." "Item to the preest of Seint Georg for hys pencion viij marcs." "Seent Georges ffest ij torches." "It. payed to iii men laboryng ii dayes in settyng up of ii yron barrs on Seynt Georges lofte ii s." "It. payed to Willm' Stayn for makeing up the mayden's ban' cloth viii d." These are scattered entries taken from the accounts of three different churches between the years 1479 and 1554. The following entry from the churchwarden's accounts of St. Laurence, Reading, is also typical:—

"1536. Charg' of Saynt George

Ffirst payd for iii caffes-skynes & ii horce skynnes, iii s vi d.
Paid for makeying the loft that Saynt George standeth upon vi d.

The Cult in England

Payd for ii plonks for the same loft viii d.
„ „ iii pesses of clowt lether ii s ii d.
„ „ makeyng the yron that the hors resteth upon vi d.
„ „ „ Saynt George's cote vii d.
„ „ John Paynter for his labour xlv s.
„ „ roses, bells, gyrdle, sword & dager iii s iiii d.
„ „ setting on the bells & roses iii d.
„ „ naylls necessary thereto x d ob.

In the reign of Henry VIII., during the religious changes, it was decided that St. George's Day should still be kept. Fabyan's Chronicle tells us that on July 22nd, 1541, "there was a proclamation that no holy daye should be kept except our Ladyes dayes, the apostle Evangelists, St. George's and St. Mary Magdalen." Eleven years after, however, in Edward VI.'s reign, we read this ominous notice in the Grey Friars Chronicle: "Item also where it hathe bene of ane olde custome that sent George shude be kepte holy day thorrow alle England, the byshoppe of London commandyd that it shudde not be kepte, and no more it was not."

Alas, the heyday of St. George's popularity was over, and after this we hear less and less of our national Saint. The gospel and epistle for St. George's Day were struck out of the Prayer Book in its revision in 1548, and even the red letter marking the 23rd April disappeared in the edition of James I.

In 1547 we read this small but significant entry on the accounts of the churchwarden of St. Martin's, Leicester: "Sold to Henry Mayblay, the horse that the George rode on, 12d:" and in 1558 it was announced in Norwich "that there be neyther George nor Margett, but for pastime the Dragon to come & shew himself as in other years." This dragon was kept until 1731, when the corporation became its owner on the dissolution of the company, and it appeared in the inventory as "item one new dragon commonly called Snap Dragon." It is now kept as a relic in the Town Museum.

The Puritans issued edicts forbidding the image of St. George to be carried in the guild processions, although they graciously gave their sanction to the dragon, which continued for many years to be a favourite. In 1610, in a procession on St. George's Day in Chester,

St. George for Merrie England

we hear of "an artificial dragon, very lively to behold" as taking part in the proceedings. Again in some Chester accounts the following entry occurs: "For the annual painting of the city's four giants, one unicorn, one dromedary, one luce, one asse, one dragon, six hobby horses, and 16 naked boys. For painting the beasts and hobby horses 43s. 0d."

From the time of the Protectorate the memory of St. George seems to have gradually faded from the minds of the people. Sometimes an effort was made to revive the interest, as when George IV. commanded that the celebrations in honour of his birthday should be transferred to St. George's Day, but it was of no avail, and the cult fell into disuse.

It is delightful, however, to find that even in these practical and prosaic times traces of old customs still linger in the country districts, reminding us of the old esteem and the old reverence. To this day boys on hobby horses parade some of the small Kentish villages on April 23, masquerading as St. George, and no doubt reaping a few pennies for their pains, and mumming plays are still given by the children of North-country villages on Christmas Eve, where, among a strange medley of characters, we again meet our old friends St. George, Sabra, the Sultan of Egypt, and the dragon.

> "O here comes I Saint George a man of Courage Bold
> And with my spear I winnd three crowns of gold.
> I slew the dragon, and brought him to the slaughter,
> And by that means I married Sabra, the beauteous
>   King of Egypt's daughter."

So run the opening lines of one of them, and throughout St. George plays the part of hero. These mumming plays are very old, and have chiefly been handed down traditionally among the country people.

Until a few years ago an old ballad called "St. George for England," was sung at Windsor on April 23rd by the choir boys of St. George's Chapel,[1] and from the time of George I. until the reign of the late Queen Victoria, a golden rose decorated the royal dining-table

---

[1] Published by Novello, price 1½d.

St. George in Literature

on the same day, the rose being the emblem of the Saint. This emblem may perhaps be traced to the sacred rose-bush which grew in the midst of the ancient churches of St. George at Urmi, which were built by the Nestorian Christians in honour of their Patron Saint. The custom of wearing a rose on April 23rd is still followed in England and the colonies, although the fashion of wearing a blue coat has long fallen into disuse. The old play of "Ram Alley," and Freeman's Epigrams of 1614 both allude to this latter fashion.

St. George is honoured in our national flag, which displays his red cross above the cross of St. Andrew, and his arms, the field argent, charged with a plain cross gules, are sometimes seen: "a bare of silver in token of clennes a crosse of goules significacion of the bloodde that Christe bleedde on ye crosse and for it muste nedes of reason by called a crosse," as John Hardyng, a chronicler of 1378, describes them. It is also interesting to know that there are 193 churches in England which are dedicated to the national saint.[1]

ST. GEORGE IN LITERATURE

A more lasting monument to St. George than the survival of old customs is the place he has taken in our literature, both in old mystery and mumming plays, and in lines by Chaucer, Drayton, Shakespeare and Spenser, and in many other old books and ballads.

The story of Una and the Red Cross Knight is only the story of St. George and Cleodolinda in one of its most fanciful and varied forms. What better description of St. George could we have than this :—

> "And on his brest a bloodie Crosse he bore,
> The deare remembrance of his dying Lord
> For whosse sweete sake that glorious badge he wore
> And dead as living, ever him ador'd :

---

[1] The Royal Society of St. George does much to keep green the memory of the Saint, and the Society of Antiquaries holds its anniversary on April 23rd. Also in 1907 the first annual service in celebration of St. George's Day was held on April 23rd, in the Chapel of the Order of St. Michael and St. George in St. Paul's Cathedral.

St. George for Merrie England

> Upon his shield the like was also scor'd
> For soveraine hope which in his help he had:
> Right faithful true he was in deede and word,
> But of his cheere did seem too solemne sad:
> Yet nothing did he dredd, but ever was ydrad."

And further on in the same book we find allusion to the English version of St. George's birth, where "Heavenly Contemplation" tells to St. George the story of his early days:—

> "For well I wote thou springs from ancient race
> Of Saxon kynges that have with mighty hand
> And many bloody battailes fought in face
> High reard their royall throne in Britans land
> And fanquisht them unable to withstand:
> From thence a faery thee unweeting reft
> There as thou slepts in tender swaddling band
> And her base Elfin brood there for thee left.
> Such men do chaungelings call so chaung'd by faeries theft.
>
> Thence she thee brought into this faery lond
> And in a heaped furrow did thee hyde;
> Where thee a ploughman all unweeting 'fond
> As he his toylesome teme that way did guyde
> And brought thee up in ploughman's state to byde
> Where of Georgos he thee gave to name,
> Till prickt with courage and thy forces pryde
> To Faery court thou cam'st to seek for fame
> And prove thy puissant arms, as seemes thee best became.
>
> . . . .
>
> For thou emongst those saints whom thou doest see
> Shalt be a saint and thine own nation's frend
> And Patrone: thou St. George shalt called bee
> Saint George of mery England, the signe of victorie."

Then in Shakespeare we find countless mention of St. George, in "Henry V." alone there being no fewer than five references. Before Harfleur, when addressing the troops, the King cries—

> "I see you stand like greyhounds in the slips
> Straining upon the start. The game's afoot;

32

St. George in Literature

> Follow your spirit, and upon the charge
> Cry 'God for Harry, England and St. George.'"

And in "Richard II.," where the King again is encouraging the soldiers—

> "Advance our standards, set upon our foes,
> Our ancient word of courage, fair St. George,
> Inspire us with the spleen of fiery dragons!
> Upon them!"

In "King John" also we get an allusion, and this time to the practice of taking the legend of St. George as a sign for inns:

> "St. George who wing'd the Dragon, and e'er since
> Sits on his horse back at mine hostess' door."

In the seventeenth century various ballads were written, all of which took the story of St. George from Richard Johnstone's version, and introduced him as an English-born saint. Two of them tell that, while awaiting the dragon, the Princess was tied to a stake, a feature of the story that is occasionally recorded in old books. These ballads are too long to quote here, but several are reprinted in Percy's "Reliques of Ancient Poetry." There was also a Chap Book which ran through many editions in the eighteenth century. It too was based on Johnstone's book, but it added a little fresh matter on its own account, and after announcing at the beginning that St. George was descended from Æneas, it ended with the startling fact that he was buried at Windsor. Its pages were greatly enlivened with curious woodcuts, not the least amusing of which presented the Princess Cleodolinda parading in a hoop.

There were also early plays and drolls in which St. George took a prominent part, and which formed part of the amusement in county houses on high days and holidays, even perhaps on long winter evenings when the time hung heavily. In one of the Paston Letters, the writer, lamenting that a man servant had left him, adds, "I have kept him thys iii yere to pleye Seynt Jage and Robin Hood and the Sheryff of Notyngham," so again we see what a familiar place the Saint held in the minds and memories of the people.

But what can be said of his place in the minds and memories of

St. George for Merrie England

the people of to-day? What have we, when all is said and done, in the legend of St. George? Surely a noble allegory which runs through the history and literature of all civilised countries, the victory of the powers of light over the powers of darkness.

Turn to the East,—in Egypt Horus kills the crocodile, in Greece Perseus slays the monster, and Belerophon overcomes the Chimera. Look to the West,—Siegfried, Sigurd, and Beowulf, all are heroes who fight with and finally overcome the most deadly monsters. On every hand the old national myths and legends, songs and sagas, tell us the same story. Change the names, vary the country, alter the circumstances, and yet the same dominating idea remains common to them all, binding them together as unconscious symbols of the growth and beliefs of many peoples. Then when the tide of Christianity swept over East and West alike, St. George with his red cross became the symbol of the power of Christ, battling with and overcoming the dragon or powers of sin, darkness, and unbelief. It is the same old story Christianised—the story of shadows fleeing before the light.

Pope Gelasius said of St. George that he was one of those saints whose names are justly reverenced among men, but whose actions are known only to God, and although St. George may be only a name to us, he has left us in his legend the finest symbol that a nation can call her own.

APPENDIX

Service for St. George's Day as used in England before the Reformation

(*Translated from the Latin of the Sarum Missal*)

Collect. O God, who causest us to rejoice in the good deeds and intercession of St. George Thy Martyr, mercifully grant that by the gift of Thy grace we may obtain the benefits we ask of him ; through . . .

Secret. We offer unto Thee, O Lord, the wonted Sacrifice on the death of Thy Martyr St. George, entreating of Thy mercy that through these holy Mysteries we may in Thy victory overcome the temptations of the Old Enemy, and of Thy bounty obtain an everlasting recompense of reward ; through . . .

P. Comm. We humbly pray Thee, Almighty Father, that we who are satisfied with the sweetness of the heavenly Table may at the intercession of Thy Martyr St. George also be partakers of His resurrection by whose death we are redeemed ; through . . .

From the Liturgy called " Typicon " formerly used in the Greek churches

O thou who art the Ransomer of the captives, the Succour of the needy, the Physician of the sick, the Defender of Princes, thou glorious Martyr George named Tropœophorus, call upon Christ to have mercy upon us.

ST. GEORGE IN ART

The following illustrations are the best testimony of how the legend of St. George has been treated in art. They show with what naïve and childlike pleasure the early artists carved and painted the story, and how its charm has been equally felt by some of the romantic painters of our own times.

As is only natural, the legend is more frequently met with in art in the countries and towns which honoured St. George as their patron at a time when their own art was vigorous. German artists for this reason have more often celebrated him than others, while in England Keyser's list of mural decorations includes over sixty frescoes and panels of St. George which have escaped the ravages of time and whitewash. This list was made, however, twenty years ago. There are also numerous other early representations in many mediums, which testify to the popularity of the cult in Pre-Reformation times. In Italian art St George is usually represented as beardless, and is often accompanied by St. Sebastian; while in German art he frequently has a beard and is often painted with St. Florian. In Gothic and French art the Saint is not so often met with, but when depicted in a group with other saints these are generally St. Maurice and St. Victor. In England St. Christopher is generally the companion saint, or sometimes St. Margaret, who also has adventures with a dragon. This is why the two saints were often represented together in processions, whereby no doubt an economy in dragons was effected, one doing duty for both. In English art St. George often wears the Garter, or else the British Lion is introduced into the scene. In Venice St. George is usually associated with St. Tryphonius, and here he must not be confused with St. Theodore and his crocodile.

When St. George is represented as fighting the dragon, but without the Princess and her parents, and the familiar background of city walls, the representation will probably be symbolic, and will be meant to celebrate the victory of Righteousness and Christianity over the powers of sin and unbelief. The dragon will be the dragon of the Apocalypse, as we read of it in the twelfth chapter: "And the great dragon was cast down, the old serpent, he that is called the Devil and Satan, the deceiver of the whole world." This symbolic representation is met with even as early as the VI. century. But when the King, Queen, and Princess are introduced, then we have the actual story of St. George. The lamb

St. George in Art

that usually accompanies the Princess is a symbol of innocence and purity, and the white horse which St. George rides has the same symbolic meaning. In Carpaccio's fine picture the horse is dark brown, but this is the only exception I know. There also is an unusual version of the story by the Master of the Calvarienberg, in which St. George has dismounted to kill the dragon, while the Princess holds the reins of the very large horse, who looks with genuine interest on the proceedings.

In old pictures and carvings St. George is almost always represented in the armour of the period in which the artist lived, and only occasionally do we find him in the classical garb of a Roman tribune; the King and Queen are generally relegated to a place on the city walls.

Through the legend in art we often catch a glimpse of the legend in history, as the last illustrations in the book will show. They prove to us how sovereigns, lords, and commoners loved to place themselves under St. George's patronage, to go down to posterity under his protection.

The illustrations can now speak for themselves. They will show how St. George and his legend has been an inspiration to many generations of artists. They will tell his story, some with delicious quaintness and sly humour, some with the dignity and the gravity that are worthy of its splendid romance.

My thanks are due to the authorities at South Kensington for their kindness and attention; to Mrs. E. Armitage for the loan of an illustration from her book "A Key to English Antiquities," which here appears on the title-page; to Messrs. Alinari (Florence), Mr. Hanfstaengl, and Mr. F. Hollyer for their kind permission to reproduce their photographs; and lastly to all whose courteous and kindly help has made my work a pleasure.

LIST OF ILLUSTRATIONS

ST. GEORGE

St. George.	*French, XV. century*	*Frontispiece*
		PAGE
St. George.	*Pisanello*	43
St. George.	*Donatello*	45
St. George.	*German, early XV. century*	47
St. George.	*Mantegna*	49
St. George.	*Dürer*	51
St. George.	*Bavarian school, early XVI. century* (?)	53

THE LEGEND

St. George armed by angels and knighted by the Virgin. *Spanish, XV. century*	57
The country people appeal to the King. *Rossetti*	59
Offerings made to appease the dragon. *Spanish, XV. century* . .	61
The drawing of lots. *Rossetti*	63
The drawing of lots. *Sir E. Burne-Jones*	65
The Princess's departure as sacrifice to the dragon. *Rossetti* . .	67
Three scenes from the life of St. George. *English, late XIV. century* .	69
Two scenes from the life of St. George. *French, XV. century* . .	71
The fight with the dragon. *German, XIV. century*	73
,, ,, ,, *Basle Cathedral, late XIV. century* . .	75
,, ,, ,, *George and Martin of Clussenburk* . .	77
,, ,, ,, *Jacopo Bellini*	79
,, ,, ,, *Crevelli*	81
,, ,, ,, *Quirico da Murano* (?)	83
,, ,, ,, *Master of the Calvarienberg* . . .	85
,, ,, ,, *Lübeck school, early XV. century* . .	87
,, ,, ,, *Sienese school, XV. century* . . .	89
,, ,, ,, *Michel Colomb*	91
,, ,, ,, *Andrea della Robbia*	93
,, ,, ,, *Bernt Notke and Hindrich Wylsynck* . .	95
,, ,, ,, *Francia*	97

List of Illustrations

		PAGE
The fight with the dragon. *Carpaccio*		99
,, ,, ,, *Raphael*		101
,, ,, ,, *Tintoretto*		103
,, ,, ,, *Rossetti*		105
,, ,, ,, *Sir E. Burne-Jones*		107
After the fight. *Pisanello*		109
St. George ties the Princess's girdle round the dragon. *Spanish, XV. century*		111
The return of St. George and the Princess. *Sir E. Burne-Jones*		113
St. George cuts off the dragon's head. *Carpaccio*		115
St. George baptizes the King, Queen, and Princess. *Altichieri and Avanzo*		117
,, ,, ,, ,, *Spanish, XV. century*		119
,, ,, ,, ,, *Carpaccio*		121
Marriage festivities of St. George and the Princess. *Rossetti*		123
St. George fights the Moors. *Spanish, XV. century*		125
St. George drinks the poisoned cup. *Spanish, XV. century*		127
St. George exorcises the demon inhabiting the idol of Apollo. *Herlen*		129
The beheading of St. George. *Altichieri and Avanzo*		131
The Vision of St. George before Antioch. *Norman, early XII. century*		133

ST. GEORGE IN A HISTORIC AND PERSONAL CONNECTION

St. George as patron of the Duke of Bedford. *Bedford Missal, 1424-1430*	137
St. George as patron of Charles the Bold. *Gerad Loyet, 1471*	139
The Sovereigns of Europe worshipping St. George. *French, circa 1490*	141
St. George as patron of the Malines Guild of Archers. *Flemish, 1495*	143
St. George as patron of Henry VII., Elizabeth of York, and family. *Engraving after Flemish (?) altar-piece, circa 1508*	145
Lucas Paumgartner as St. George. *Dürer*	147
St. George as patron of an unknown donor. *Flemish, circa 1510*	149
Procession of the Guild of St. Gudula, Brussels. *Van Alsloot*	151
Charles I. and Henrietta Maria as St. George and the Princess. *Rubens*	153
The children of the Duke of Bedford as St. George, the Princess, and attendants. *Sir J. Reynolds*	155

The line engraving on the title-page is from a Norman tombstone at Conisborough.

ST. GEORGE

"The blessyd George was hygh in despysing lowe thynges, and therfore he haa verdeur in hym self, he was attemperate by dyscressyon and therfore he had wyn of gladnesse, and wythin he was playne of humylite, and therby put he forth whete of good werke." —GOLDEN LEGEND.

ST. GEORGE

Pisanello (circa 1385–1455). Part of a picture in
the National Gallery.

ST. GEORGE

Donatello (1386-1466). Bargello, Florence.

ST. GEORGE

German School. Early XV. century. National Museum, Nuremberg.

ST. GEORGE

Mantegna (1431-1506). Accademia, Venice.

ST. GEORGE

Dürer (1471-1528). From the engraving.

ST. GEORGE

Bavarian School. Early XVI. century (?). Frauen Kirche, Munich.

THE LEGEND

ST. GEORGE ARMED BY ANGELS AND KNIGHTED BY THE VIRGIN
From a Spanish altar-piece. XV. century. South Kensington Museum.

THE COUNTRY PEOPLE APPEAL TO THE KING

D. G. Rossetti (1828-1882). From a design for a window in the collection of Mr. Fairfax Murray.

F. Hollyer, photo.

OFFERINGS MADE TO APPEASE THE DRAGON

From a Spanish altar-piece.   XV. century.   South Kensington Museum.

F. Hoyer, photo.

THE DRAWING OF LOTS

D. G. Rossetti (1828–1882). From a water-colour sketch for a window in the collection of Mr. Fairfax Murray.

THE DRAWING OF LOTS
Sir E. Burne-Jones (1833-1898).

F. Hollyer, photo.

THE PRINCESS'S DEPARTURE AS SACRIFICE TO THE DRAGON

D. G. Rossetti (1828-1882). From a design for a window in the collection of Mr. Fairfax Murray.

THREE SCENES FROM THE LIFE OF ST. GEORGE

English. Late XIV. century. South Kensington Museum.

This panel—part of a chest—is said to have come from Rufford Abbey. Notice the British Lion; also the King and Queen in the tower

69

TWO SCENES FROM THE LIFE OF ST. GEORGE

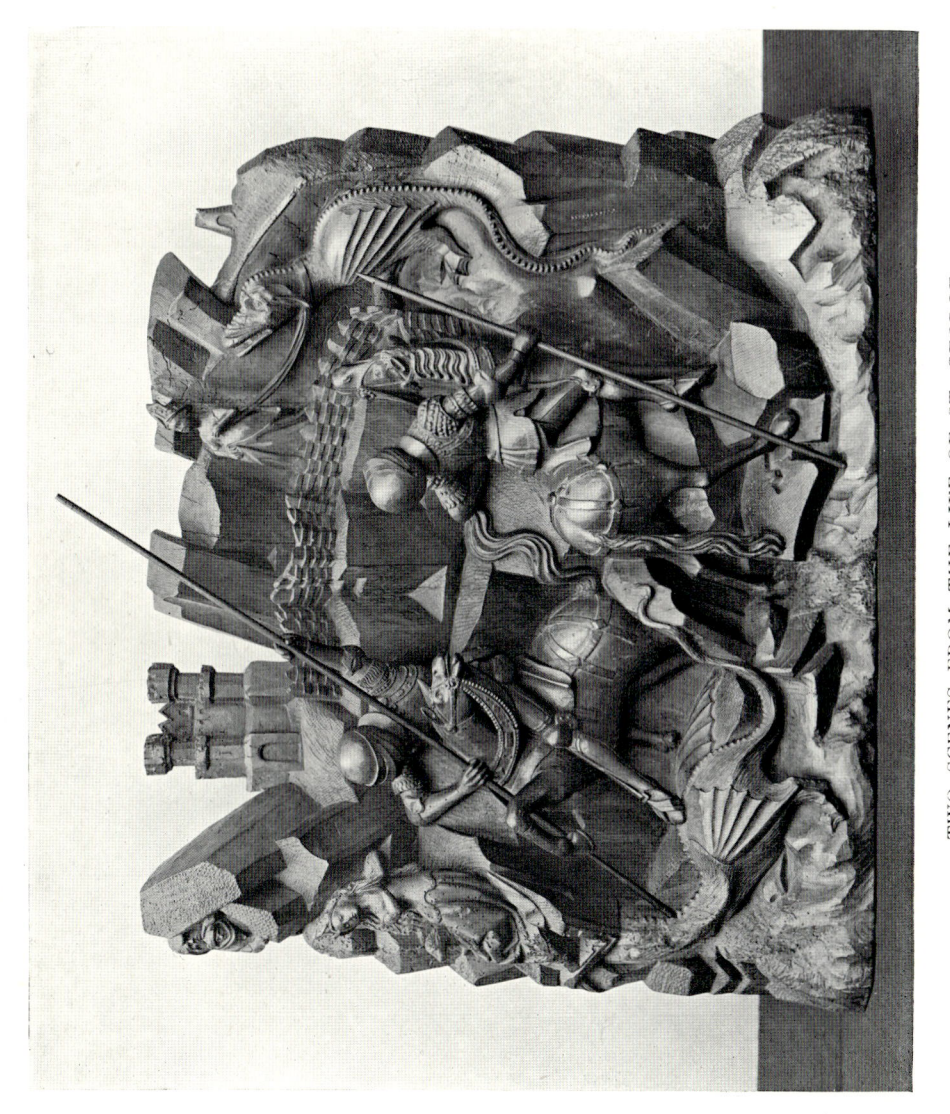

French. XV. century. South Kensington Museum. From the collection of Mr. Salting.

THE FIGHT WITH THE DRAGON

German water ewer. XIV. century. Bargello, Florence.

THE FIGHT WITH THE DRAGON
Second half XIV. century, restored 1372. Basle Cathedral.

THE FIGHT WITH THE DRAGON

George & Martin of Clussenburk. Hungarian School, 1373. From a fountainhead in the Palace Court, Prague.

THE FIGHT WITH THE DRAGON

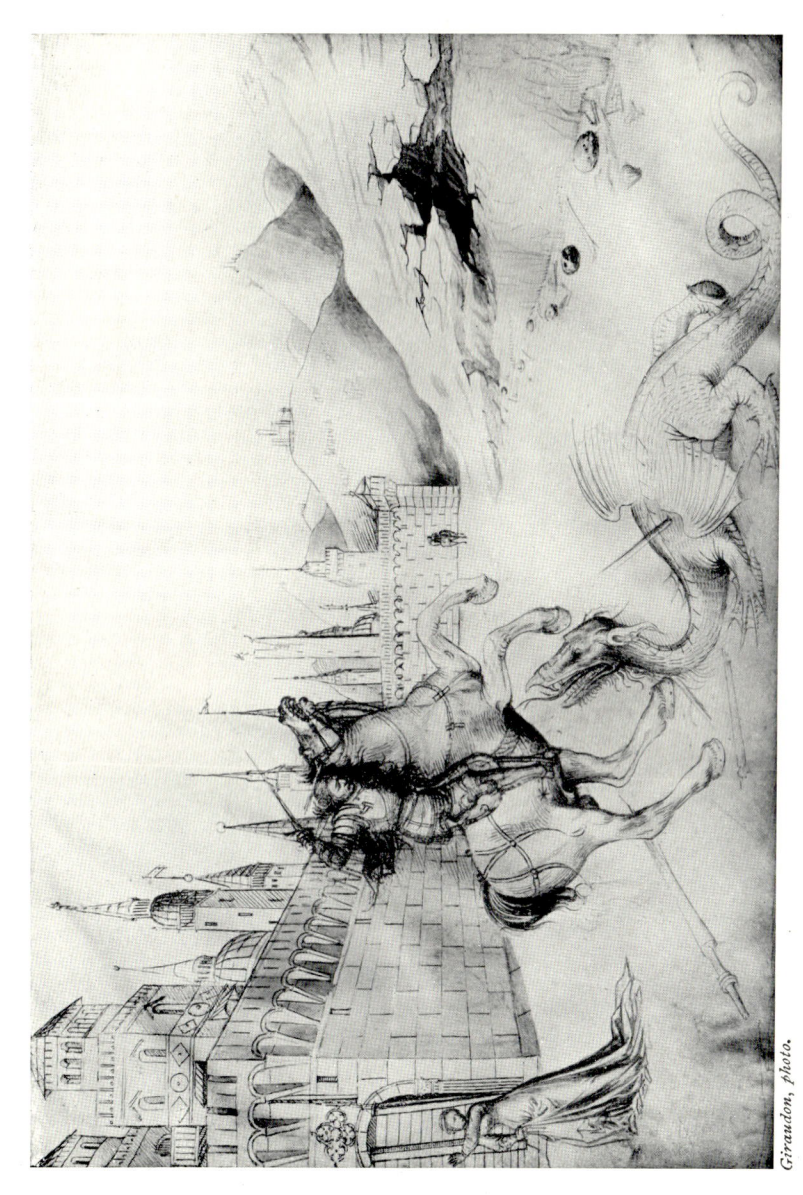

Jacopo Bellini (active 1430–1470). From a drawing in the Louvre.

Giraudon, photo.

THE FIGHT WITH THE DRAGON

Crevelli (1430-after 1493). From collection of Mrs. Gardner, Boston.

THE FIGHT WITH THE DRAGON

Quirico da Murano (?). XV. century. Martinengo Gallery, Brescia.

THE FIGHT WITH THE DRAGON
Master of the Calvarienberg (circa 1450). From the engraving.

THE FIGHT WITH THE DRAGON

Lübeck School.   Early XV. century.   Lübeck Museum.

THE FIGHT WITH THE DRAGON

Sienese School. XV. century. Siena.

THE FIGHT WITH THE DRAGON
Michel Colomb (circa 1431-1511). Louvre.

Alinari, *photo.*

THE FIGHT WITH THE DRAGON

Andrea della Robbia (1435-1517). Church of Sta. Maria and S. Giorgio, Brancoli.

Jaeger, photo.

THE FIGHT WITH THE DRAGON

Bernt Notke and Hindrich Wylsynck (Lübeck School, 1480). Historical Museum, Stockholm.

This group was commissioned by the Swedes as a thank-offering after a successful battle against the Danes in 1471. The victory was attributed to the intervention of St. George when called upon by the Swedes. The breast of the figure contains relics which were presented by the Pope when the group was completed.

THE FIGHT WITH THE DRAGON
Francia (1450-1517). Corsini Gallery, Rome.

THE FIGHT WITH THE DRAGON
Carpaccio (active 1478-1522). Church of San Giorgio di Schiavoni, Venice.

THE FIGHT WITH THE DRAGON

Raphael (1483-1520). Hermitage Gallery, St. Petersburg.

Presented to Henry VII. by the Duke of Urbino on the occasion of his being made a Knight of the Garter. Notice the Garter worn by St. George.

THE FIGHT WITH THE DRAGON
Tintoretto (1512–1594).   National Gallery.

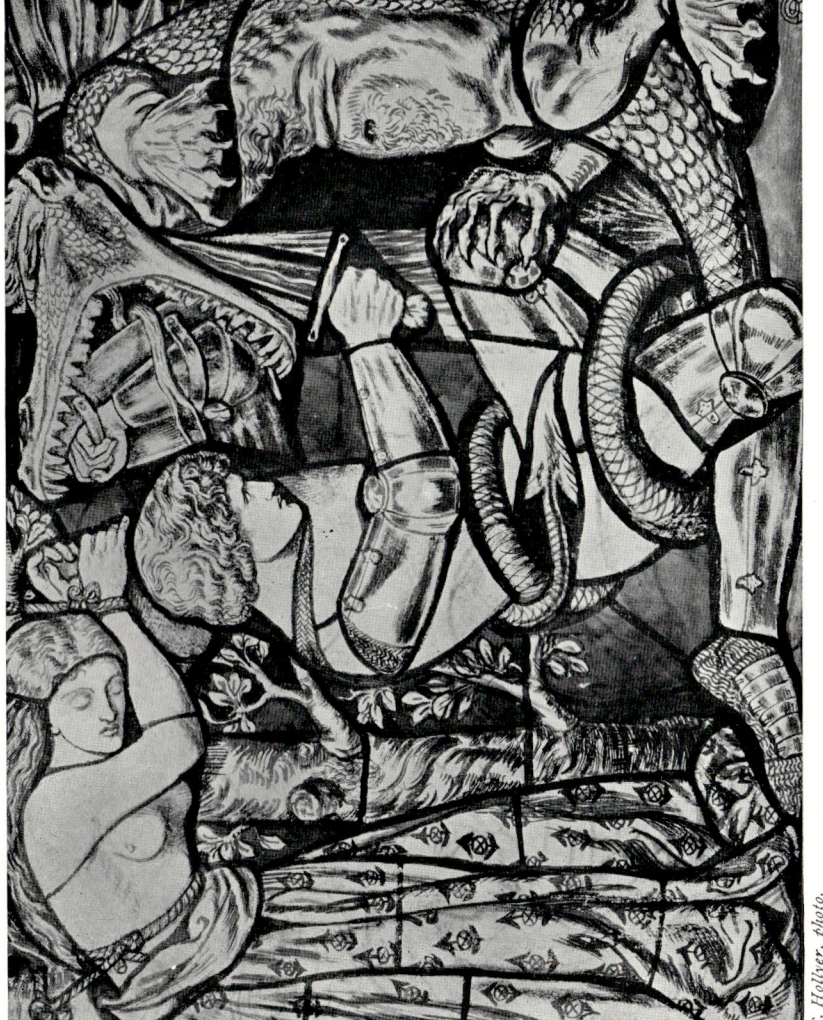

THE FIGHT WITH THE DRAGON. From a design for a window in the collection of Mr. Fairfax Murray.

D. G. Rossetti (1828-1882).

THE FIGHT WITH THE DRAGON
Sir E. Burne-Jones (1833-1898).

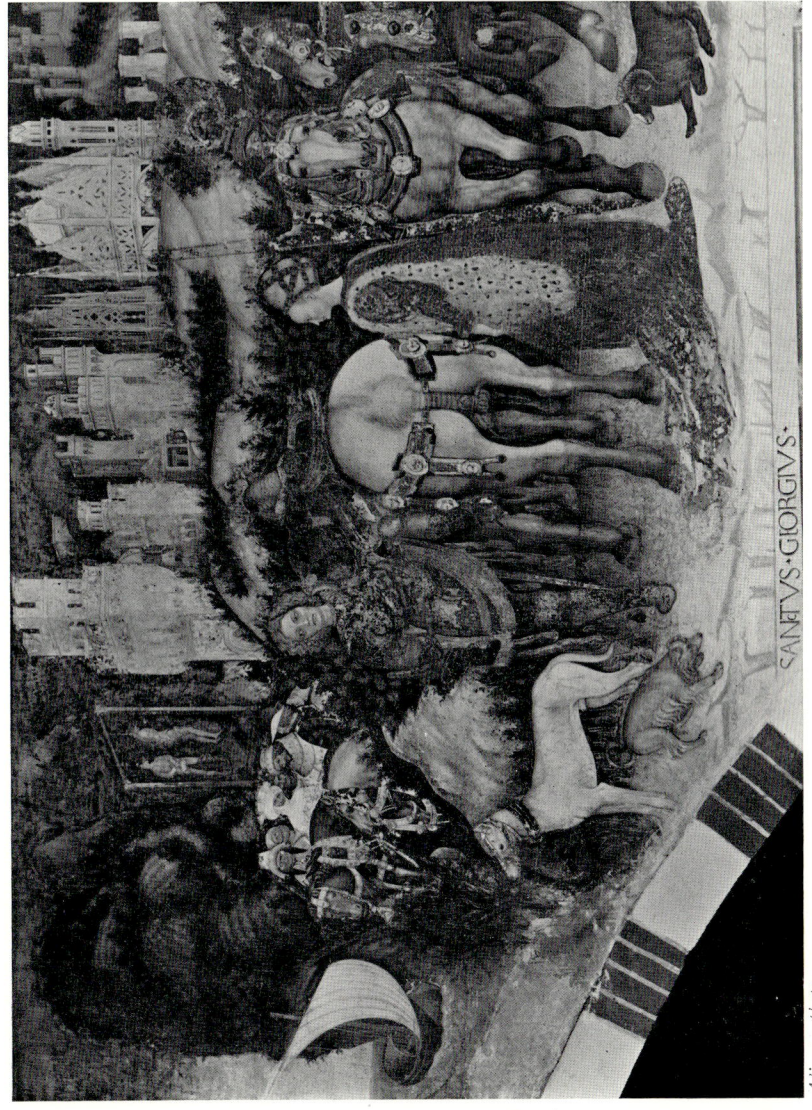

AFTER THE FIGHT

Pisanello (circa 1385-1455). Church of St. Anastasia, Verona.

ST. GEORGE TIES THE PRINCESS'S GIRDLE ROUND
THE DRAGON

From a Spanish altar-piece. XV. century. South Kensington Museum.

THE RETURN OF ST. GEORGE AND THE PRINCESS

Sir E. Burne-Jones (1833–1898).

ST. GEORGE CUTS OFF THE DRAGON'S HEAD

Carpaccio (active 1478-1522). Church of San Giorgio di Schiavoni, Venice.

ST. GEORGE BAPTIZES THE KING, QUEEN, AND PRINCESS
Altichieri and Avanzo. Late XIV. century. Chapel of St. George, Padua.

ST. GEORGE BAPTIZES THE KING, QUEEN, AND PRINCESS
From a Spanish altar-piece.   XV. century.   South Kensington Museum.

ST. GEORGE BAPTIZES THE KING, QUEEN, AND PRINCESS
Carpaccio (active 1478-1522). Church of San Giorgio di Schiavoni, Venice.
See also Plate No. LXI., Vol. XXIV., of "The Life, Letters, and Works of Ruskin."

MARRIAGE FESTIVITIES OF ST. GEORGE AND THE PRINCESS
D. G. Rossetti (1828–1882). From a design for a window in the collection of Mr. Fairfax Murray.

ST. GEORGE FIGHTS THE MOORS

From a Spanish altar-piece. XV. century. South Kensington Museum.

ST. GEORGE DRINKS THE POISONED CUP
(In the foreground the beheading of St. George).
From a Spanish altar-piece. XV. century. South Kensington Museum.

ST. GEORGE EXORCISES THE DEMON INHABITING
THE IDOL OF APOLLO

F. Herlen. Last half of XV. century. Town Museum, Nördlingen.

THE BEHEADING OF ST. GEORGE

Altichieri and Avanzo. Late XIV. century. Chapel of St. George, Padua.

Walton Adams, photo.

THE VISION OF ST. GEORGE BEFORE ANTIOCH

Norman (circa 1140). Fordington Church, Dorset.

St. George here figures as the Champion of Christendom. The Crusaders kneel in prayer to the left. To the right the Saracens are overcome by the Saint. (See p. 21.)

ST. GEORGE IN A HISTORIC AND PERSONAL CONNECTION

ST. GEORGE AS PATRON OF THE DUKE OF BEDFORD
From the Bedford Missal (1424-1430).

St. George here wears the Garter on his left leg, and the long blue mantle of the Order of the Garter, with its cords, tassels, and badge. The Duke of Bedford (brother of Henry V. and a Knight of the Garter) is mentioned on p. 25 as attending a feast of St. George at Windsor. In Henry VI. (Part I. Act i. scene 1) Shakespeare makes him say—

"Farewell, my masters; to my task will I;
Bonfires in France forthwith I am to make,
To keep our great St. George's feast withal."

ST. GEORGE AS PATRON OF CHARLES THE BOLD

Gerad Loyet of Bruges (1471).

Given by Charles to the Church of St. Jaques, Liège, "in expiation of the horrors committed in the sack of this town" (in 1468). His stall plate, as a Knight of the Garter, is still to be seen in the Chapel of St. George, Windsor.

THE SOVEREIGNS OF EUROPE WORSHIPPING ST. GEORGE

From a French miniature, circa 1490.

The figure to the right is Henry VII., King of England. The one behind him is Ferdinand, King of Spain. In the centre kneels the Emperor Frederic III., and behind him are Maximilian, King of the Romans, and further to the right Philip, Archduke of Austria and Duke of Burgundy. In the foreground to the left kneels Charles VIII., King of France.

ST. GEORGE AS PATRON OF THE MALINES GUILD OF ARCHERS
1495. Royal Museum, Antwerp.

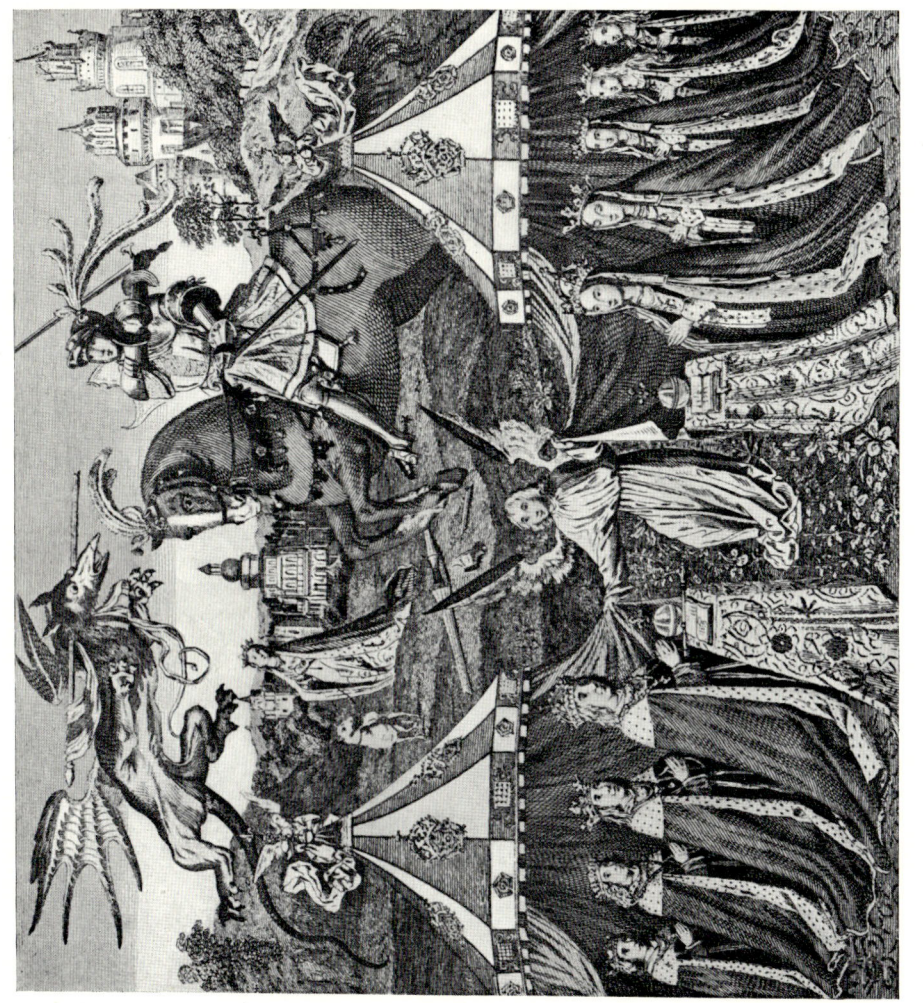

ST. GEORGE AS PATRON OF HENRY VII., ELIZABETH OF YORK, AND FAMILY

Windsor Castle in background.

From Grignion's engraving after a Flemish (?) altar-piece, circa 1508.   Collection of H.M. the King, Windsor.

LUCAS PAUMGARTNER AS ST. GEORGE

Dürer (1471-1528). Alt Pinakothek, Munich.

ST. GEORGE AS PATRON OF AN UNKNOWN DONOR

Flemish (circa 1510). Munich Gallery.

PROCESSION OF THE GUILD OF ST. GUDULA, BRUSSELS

With figures representing St. George, the Dragon, and the Princess.

D. van Alsloot. Early XVII. century (?). Brussels Gallery.

CHARLES I. AND HENRIETTA MARIA AS ST. GEORGE AND THE PRINCESS
Rubens (1577-1640). Collection of H.M. the King, Buckingham Palace.

THE CHILDREN OF THE DUKE OF BEDFORD AS ST. GEORGE, THE PRINCESS,
AND ATTENDANTS

Sir J. Reynolds (1723-1792).   From an engraving.